The Lit of Clay an Materials

'Hands on' creativity

by Lorraine Frankish

Illustrations by Martha Hardy

LITTLE BOOKS WITH BIG IDEAS

Featherstone Education
An imprint of Bloomsbury Publishing Plc

50 Bedford Square
London
WC1B 3DP
UK

1385 Broadway
New York
NY 10018
USA

www.bloomsbury.com

Bloomsbury is a registered trade mark of Bloomsbury Publishing Plc

First published 2005
This second edition published 2014

Text © Lorraine Frankish, 2005
Illustrations © Matha Hardy
Series editor: Sally Featherstone

British Library Cataloguing-in-Publication Data
A catalogue record for this book is available from the British Library.

ISBN: 978-1-4729-1416-3

Library of Congress Cataloging-in-Publication Data
A catalog record for this book is available from the Library of Congress.

1 3 5 7 9 10 8 6 4 2

Printed and bound in India by Replika Press Pvt. Ltd

This book is produced using paper that is made from wood grown in managed, sustainable forests. It is natural, renewable and recyclable. The logging and manufacturing processes conform to the environmental regulations of the country of origin.

To view more of our titles please visit www.bloomsbury.com

Contents

Introduction 4
Clay day 10
Clay together, play together 12
Little lights 14
Shapes and letters 16
Thumbs up! Thumbs down! 18
Wet clay play 20
Make an impression 22
Hands-on printing 24
Material world 26
Measure for measure 28
Making models 30
Beside the seaside 32
Glorious mud! 34
Snow 36
Soap snow 38
Craft clay 40
Cornflour magic 42
Finger paint 44
Squirty cream 46
Shiny, slimy soap flakes 48
Bean feast! 50
Spaghetti or jelly 52
Breakfast cereals 54
Compost 56
Toilet tissue medium 58
Porridge 60
Sawdust 62
Paper pulp 64
Making magic 66
Wire sculpture 68
Turf 70
Gravel 72
Very tiny seeds 74
Dots and strips 76
Icy shapes 78

Introduction

This book is one of the titles in a series of Little Books, which explore aspects of practice within the Early Years Foundation Stage in England. The books are also suitable for practitioners working with the early years curriculum in Wales, Northern Ireland and Scotland, and in any early years setting catering for young children.

Across the series you will find titles appropriate to each aspect of the curriculum for children from two to five years, giving practitioners a wealth of ideas for engaging activities, interesting resources and stimulating environments to enrich their work across the early years curriculum.

Each title also has information linking the activity pages to the statutory early years curriculum for England. This title has been updated to include the revised Early Learning Goals published by the Department for Education in March 2012. The full set of 19 goals is included in the introduction to each book, and the activity pages will refer you to the relevant statements to which each activity contributes.

For the purposes of observation and assessment of the children's work in each activity, we recommend that practitioners should use each of the 'revised statements' as a whole, resisting any impulse to separate the elements of each one into short phrases.

The key goals for this title are highlighted in green, although other goals may be included on some pages.

PRIME AREAS

Communication and language

1 **Listening and attention:** children listen attentively in a range of situations. They listen to stories, accurately anticipating key events and respond to what they hear with relevant comments, questions or actions. They give their attention to what others say and respond appropriately, while engaged in another activity.

2 **Understanding:** children follow instructions involving several ideas or actions. They answer 'how' and 'why' questions about their experiences and in response to stories or events.

3 **Speaking:** children express themselves effectively, showing awareness of listeners' needs. They use past, present and future forms accurately when talking about events that have happened or are to happen in the future. They develop their own narratives and explanations by connecting ideas or events.

Physical development

(1) Moving and handling: children show good control and co-ordination in large and small movements. They move confidently in a range of ways, safely negotiating space. They handle equipment and tools effectively, including pencils for writing.

(2) Health and self-care: children know the importance for good health of physical exercise, and a healthy diet, and talk about ways to keep healthy and safe. They manage their own basic hygiene and personal needs successfully, including dressing and going to the toilet independently.

Personal, social and emotional development

(1) Self-confidence and self-awareness: children are confident to try new activities, and say why they like some activities more than others. They are confident to speak in a familiar group, will talk about their ideas, and will choose the resources they need for their chosen activities. They say when they do or don't need help.

(2) Managing feelings and behaviour: children talk about how they and others show feelings, talk about their own and others' behaviour, and its consequences, and know that some behaviour is unacceptable. They work as part of a group or class, and understand and follow the rules. They adjust their behaviour to different situations, and take changes of routine in their stride.

(3) Making relationships: children play co-operatively, taking turns with others. They take account of one another's ideas about how to organise their activity. They show sensitivity to others' needs and feelings, and form positive relationships with adults and other children.

SPECIFIC AREAS

Literacy

(1) Reading: children read and understand simple sentences. They use phonic knowledge to decode regular words and read them aloud accurately. They also read some common irregular words. They demonstrate understanding when talking with others about what they have read.

(2) Writing: children use their phonic knowledge to write words in ways which match their spoken sounds. They also write some irregular common words. They write simple sentences which can be read by themselves and others. Some words are spelt correctly and others are phonetically plausible.

Mathematics

(1) Numbers: children count reliably with numbers from 1 to 20, place them in order and say which number is one more or one less than a given number. Using quantities and objects, they add and subtract two single-digit numbers and count on or back to find the answer. They solve problems, including doubling, halving and sharing.

(2) Shape, space and measures: children use everyday language to talk about size, weight, capacity, position, distance, time and money to compare quantities and objects and to solve problems. They recognise, create and describe patterns. They explore characteristics of everyday objects and shapes and use mathematical language to describe them.

Understanding the world

(1) People and communities: children talk about past and present events in their own lives and in the lives of family members. They know that other children don't always enjoy the same things, and are sensitive to this. They know about similarities and differences between themselves and others, and among families, communities and traditions.

(2) The world: children know about similarities and differences in relation to places, objects, materials and living things. They talk about the features of their own immediate environment and how environments might vary from one another. They make observations of animals and plants and explain why some things occur, and talk about changes.

(3) Technology: children recognise that a range of technology is used in places such as homes and schools. They select and use technology for particular purposes.

Expressive arts and design

(1) Exploring and using media and materials: children sing songs, make music and dance, and experiment with ways of changing them. They safely use and explore a variety of materials, tools and techniques, experimenting with colour, design, texture, form and function.

(2) Being imaginative: children use what they have learnt about media and materials in original ways, thinking about uses and purposes. They represent their own ideas, thoughts and feelings through design and technology, art, music, dance, role-play and stories.

This Little Book offers practitioners step-by-step activities for using clay and other malleable materials with children in the Foundation Stage. All the activities make use of materials and equipment that can be found in the setting or bought easily and cheaply, and will need little preparation.

The self-hardening clay suggested is good to manipulate and shape, and is air-drying, so it does not need to be fired in a kiln. It can be bought from craft shops and educational suppliers.

The activities can be messy, but with a little preparation will not be too difficult to manage. Involve the children in clearing away and they won't see this as a chore, just another enjoyable activity.

Washable surfaces are ideal, but if this is not possible, cover tables with plastic sheets or newspapers.

Before starting any of the activities, it is important that you are fully aware of any children who have allergies or may need extra assistance. For example, a child's eczema will be irritated when playing with a finger paint that contains salt, so they will need to wear gloves.

Children should be able to work independently through most of the suggested steps, although at first, younger children may need help to master some of the skills. Practitioners should interact and offer support in developing confidence and independence, extending language and thinking and ensuring that health and safety standards are maintained.

When children play with clay and other malleable materials, they will be experiencing a variety of textures and smells. They will be discovering how these materials respond and experimenting with shape and form. Children will have the opportunity to acquire new skills and techniques while developing their concentration, hand and eye co-ordination and creativity.

Children will need:

▶ sufficient quantity to allow them to explore the materials. As a guide, each child will require a lump of clay at least the size of a grapefruit.

▶ enough space to be able to manipulate clay or other materials.

▶ sufficient time to explore and experiment with ideas, materials and activities.

When encountering activities for the first time, some children may be reluctant to take part straight away and will need time and encouragement before they join in. However, exploring clay and other natural substances can be relaxing and help children to release their emotional energy.

The activities are child-centred, encouraging children to experiment and explore, providing opportunities for growth in many skills and helping build children's confidence, as there is not a right or wrong way to carry them out.

A few activities do have a suggested end result, but even in these activities children should be encouraged to express their own creativity, for example, by choosing what colour to paint a pot or how to decorate it.

Practitioners should value children's own ideas and not expect them to reproduce someone else's picture, dance, model or recipe.

Clay day

Clay is great for exploring, poking, pummelling and rolling – there's no need to rush into using tools or making a particular object.

What you need:

- a lump of clay for each child (you could use self-hardening clay, but ordinary clay is cheaper, easier to handle and a better texture for beginners)
- boards, or squares of hessian (sacking) to work on
- small plastic jugs or cups of water.

Suggestions:

- You can buy clay (in basic or self-hardening varieties) from educational catalogues, or by shopping on line. Make sure the clay is intended for use by children, and invest in several different sorts and colours.

What you do:

Free play is a vital introduction to clay work, allowing children to explore and experiment as they get used to the texture and what clay can do. Spend time with the children as they work, exploring the texture of the clay. Discuss how it is like dough, but different, and that the children can play with it freely without 'making' anything.

1. Place the hessian squares or base boards on a low table.

2. Add a lump of clay for each child.

3. Invite the children to play with the clay.

4. Don't be tempted to make models for the children to copy, just play alongside.

5. Make holes in the clay and add a little water from the jugs if it begins to get dry and difficult to work.

6. When the children have finished, pile the clay together and cover with plastic or a very wet cloth until other children show an interest.

7. Spray or splash the clay with water and store it in an airtight container (a plastic ice cream tub is ideal). Clay will keep indefinitely, but may dry out if left for a time. In this case, poke holes in the clay lump with a pencil or stick, and fill the holes with water and leave overnight before using it.

More little ideas...

▶ Put all of the clay in the middle of the table and let the children divide it themselves. Add some plastic or blunt knives (such as butter knives).

▶ Set up the clay outdoors on the ground on a plastic sheet.

Clay together, play together

Children love playing with clay when it is presented in this way. They will be learning to take turns, negotiating and playing co-operatively.

What you need:

▶ a large bag of clay

▶ a jug of water (or a watering can) to keep the clay moist

▶ a plastic sheet or a builder's tray – big enough for four children to play comfortably

▶ tools such as plastic knives, spoons and lolly sticks

▶ twigs.

Suggestions:

▶ Invest in a builder's tray. You will find endless uses for it and, when not in use it, will slide neatly behind a cupboard or under a table.

▶ Use carpet samples or carpet tiles for children to sit on, especially if working outside.

▶ Remember that playing together with one big lump of clay is difficult for some children, who will want to cut off their own piece. Work with them and explain that this is a group activity.

What you do:

1. Make sure the children are wearing protective clothing – this is a really messy activity!

2. Put the plastic sheet or tray on the floor, indoors or outside.

3. Put the big lump of clay in the centre of the sheet.

4. Make sure the children have access to the tools. Put some on each corner to make access easier.

5. Ask a small group (of about four) to work and play together, keeping the clay as a whole piece.

6. Stay close so you can help or guide the discussion as the children work – some may need reminding to work together.

More little ideas...

▶ Set up the clay outside on a fairly level surface in a shady spot or under a gazebo.

▶ Give the children small world toys, such as plastic people, vehicles or animals and let them use the clay as a base for their imaginative play.

▶ Provide a big bowl of soapy water for washing the toys when they have finished. The children will love this extra activity and it will make sure their hands are really clean!

Little lights

Divas are small lamps that are lit for celebrations, especially at Diwali, the Hindu festival of light, celebrated in October or November each year.

What you need:

▶ a ball of clay about the size of a tennis ball for each child
▶ rolling pins, a circular pastry cutter, plastic knives or butter knives
▶ a hand spray filled with water
▶ card and pen for labels
▶ a tea light candle for each child.

Suggestions:

▶ You could carry out this activity as part of a topic on light or celebrations. Talk about Diwali and read or tell some relevant stories.

▶ Before starting the activity, make sure you warn the children of the dangers of candles and matches. Always keep these out of reach of the children unless they are carefully and constantly supervised.

What you do:

1. Give each child a lump of clay.

2. Show them how to roll the clay into a ball. Then help them to roll their clay flat using the rolling pins.

3. Cut a circle out of the clay using the pastry cutter or a blunt knife.

4. Using both hands, turn the edges of the circle up. The diva should be the shape of a boat, with pointed bits at each end. Some children may find this difficult, so let them have another go if they need it, or take a relaxed attitude to the final shape! Spray the clay with water if it starts to dry out from over-handling.

5. Show them how to smooth the shape with their fingers.

6. Press down gently on the diva to flatten the base so that it is stable and won't fall over or wobble. Clay is very forgiving and will take any amount of reshaping as long as you keep it damp.

7. Give each child a piece of card to make their own name label.

8. Put the divas on the labels and leave to dry in an area where they will not be disturbed.

9. Leave to dry for approximately 48 hours before putting a tea light candle inside each diva.

More little ideas...

▶ Before the clay is dry, decorate the divas with patterns by marking with sticks or clay tools.

▶ Paint the divas with a mixture of paint and white glue, and add some glitter or sequins before the paint dries.

Shapes and letters

Making sausages, rolls, spirals and twists of clay is a stage most children go through in exploring what clay can do. Use this natural interest to help children to strengthen their fingers and hands as they explore.

What you need:

► a ball of clay for each child
► a board or hessian square each
► rolling pins
► shape templates (see next page).

I will need

Suggestions:

► Younger or less experienced children need plenty of time to explore this activity without direction or templates. If they seem to need help, just sit with them and make some shapes yourself.

► For more confident children, make some simple templates (spirals, zigzags, snakes etc.) by drawing shapes on card with a thick marker and then laminating the cards to protect them from the damp clay.

You may wish to copy the following patterns for your templates:

What you do:

1. Work alongside the children, rolling, shaping and twisting the 'sausages' into different shapes and patterns. Younger children could make spirals, circles, straight shapes and 's' shapes in preparation for letter-making later.

2. When the children have had plenty of free exploration (this may take many sessions over time), introduce the templates and talk about the shapes and patterns before introducing the idea of making letters.

3. Talk about the shapes together and ask the children to choose a template they like. Then they can follow the form of the letter in clay by shaping the sausages to the template lines.

More little ideas...

▶ Older or more experienced children may enjoy making letter and number shapes, or even whole words. You could use plastic or wooden numbers and letters as templates. Make sure they are big enough – small shapes will be much less satisfying.

▶ When finished and dried, the letters could be painted and varnished to make a collage or name plates.

Thumbs up! Thumbs down!

These little pots are easy to make and children will love creating them, even if they are only used for the session to fill with clay beads or other play items.

What you need:

► a small ball of clay each
► a board or hessian square each
► water in a hand sprayer
► card for names.

I will need

Suggestions:

► Make clay a part of everyday life by offering it on a very regular basis. Let children know that working with these malleable materials does not involve a 'finished article'. Take time to sit with them and experience the fun of just playing!

► Clay thumb pots are a good accessory in play. They can be filled with smaller items also made from clay. Experiment with the children in making little balls, snakes, strips, squares etc. Provide some safe knives to cut the shapes.

What you do:

1. Share out the clay so everyone has a piece about the size of a tennis ball.

2. Roll the clay into a ball and, holding it in one hand, push the thumb of the other hand into the clay ball. Turn the clay in your hand as you push your thumb into the ball, gradually making a bigger and bigger hole, and working the sides out from the middle. Remind the children not to let the sides get too thin.

   If the clay gets dry and starts to crack, moisten it with water from the spray bottle.

3. You may not want to keep the little pots after the children have played with them. If you do, you could:

   ▷ make patterns in the pots with clay tools, sticks or wooden skewers and then:

   ▷ paint self-hardening clay with hardener and leave to dry before painting with a mixture of paint and white glue;

   ▷ leave basic clay for 48 hours before painting these with the same mixture.

More little ideas...

▶ Make a list together of all the things children can do with their fingers and thumbs.

▶ Go outdoors and fill the pot with small natural objects, such as seeds, pebbles or leaves. Later, ask the children to empty their pot and look at the things they have collected. Talk about each item.

Wet clay play

Adding water to clay quickly changes its consistency and feel. very wet clay is both a sensory and a creative activity. Encourage the children to explore what it can do as they poke and pummel it.

What you need:

▶ a bag of clay
▶ a large tray, a baby bath or a water trolley
▶ small plastic jugs, bottles and hand sprays
▶ newspaper or a supply of old towels.

Suggestions:

▶ This activity is much better done outdoors – then the children can really enjoy the experience without your anxiety about mess and spills. An outdoor source of water would also be welcome, as the children will never have enough!

▶ Use a hose to clean the ground when the children have finished playing. They will be very keen to help.

What you do: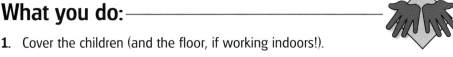

1. Cover the children (and the floor, if working indoors!).

2. Some children may find it difficult at first to pour the water a little at a time, so give them a small amount and let them refill their jugs frequently. Offer sprays and other water containers as well.

3. Put the clay into the tray.

4. As the children begin to play with the clay, talk about how it feels, looks and slides.

5. Encourage the children to use descriptive words, such as 'slimy', 'sliding', 'shiny', 'slippery' and 'liquid', and let them explore the clay, pummelling and poking it until it begins to dry.

6. Pour some water on to the clay a little at a time, and work it in, moving it around, squeezing, pressing and twisting it.

7. Talk about how the clay changes.

8. Continue to add water until the clay is very soft – almost liquid.

9. If the clay gets too runny, leave it for a while in a sunny place. Encourage the children to keep watching it to see what happens.

More little ideas...

▶ Put all the clay in the middle of the table or tray and let the children divide it into pieces themselves.

▶ Make holes and tunnels in the clay by pushing in fingers and thumbs or using tools.

▶ Leave the tray of clay in the room for several days and watch what happens as it dries out and hardens.

Make an impression

Create some interesting patterns by pressing a collection of objects into damp clay. The more unusual the object, the more surprising the result, so start experimenting!

What you need:

► a lump of clay for each child

► a collection of small objects – buttons, pebbles, coins, leaves, spools, sticks, fir cones, shells, Lego bricks etc.

► a small bowl of water for rinsing objects

► rolling pins.

Suggestions:

► The children could help with collecting objects. Look indoors and in the garden for objects that are small and have interesting textures. You could go on a 'feeling walk' to collect some more things.

► Make sure the clay is fairly moist and soft so the objects make a good impression.

What you do:

1. Give each child a lump of clay and let them use their hands or a rolling pin to flatten it on a board or some hessian.

2. Now look at the objects you have collected together and invite the children to choose a few to try.

3. Experiment with pressing the objects into the clay. Look at the patterns they make.

4. Compare the print in the clay with the shape of the object.

5. Continue to print with the objects, making random or repeat patterns.

6. When the children have made some patterns, roll the clay into a ball again and flatten and smooth with hands or rolling pins.

7. Change objects and repeat the activity. You can keep the textured pieces or treat it as an experiential activity.

8. Let the children help you to clean the objects in a bowl of water. Watch the clay wash off and change the colour of the water.

More little ideas...

▶ Look in your kitchen for more interesting texture items – sieves, a potato masher, a garlic press, a colander, a washing-up brush or pan scourer and a grater.

▶ Some fabrics make good textures; try lace, hessian or netting.

▶ Use the same objects to print with paint and compare the patterns. Take some photos, mount them on card and laminate them to make a texture-matching game.

▶ Look at textures and patterns indoors and outdoors, such as shoe soles, brickwork, drain covers and leaves.

Hands-on printing

This classic activity makes a wonderful keepsake for children, parents and grandparents.

What you need:

▶ a lump of clay for each child

▶ a margarine container big enough for a child's hand to fit into (Vitalite round tubs are good)

▶ water to keep clay moist

▶ plaster of Paris (available from educational suppliers and craft shops)

▶ a jug, labels and newspaper.

Suggestions:

▶ This activity is suitable for two or three children at a time, not more.

▶ Remember that plaster of Paris hardens very quickly, You need to be absolutely ready for the crucial stage before you add water to the plaster.

▶ Check for any allergies or children with eczema before doing this activity. For any susceptible children, provide thin polythene gloves or cover the plaster with cling film.

What you do:

1. Help the children to press moist clay into the bottom of a margarine container so that it is deeper than the child's hand.

2. Using your fingers, help the children to smooth the surface of the clay.

3. Invite the children to press their hands into the clay, encouraging them to spread their fingers first.

4. Suggest that they press down firmly so that they make a deep impression.

5. Look at the impression, discussing the lines and markings they have made. Look together at the child's hand, spotting the marks and lines there. Use a magnifying glass if you have one.

6. Following the instructions on the packet, mix up the plaster of Paris in a large jug. The children will need help with this as it begins to set quite quickly. Remind the children not to touch the plaster.

7. Before the plaster begins to set, pour it on to the clay handprint, making sure that it is covered to at least 1cm thick.

8. Label each tub and leave to set for a few hours.

9. Remove the cast from the margarine container and clean off any clay from the plaster by holding it under gently running water.

10. When the cast is dry, write the child's name and the date on the back.

11. The clay can be reused for another activity.

More little ideas...

► Draw a picture in the clay with a wooden skewer or sharp pencil and then make a cast with plaster of Paris.

► Make clay handprints and compare these with the plaster casts.

Material world

Adding things to clay helps to develop thinking and creativity.
Offer a mixture of sizes of objects to help hand-eye co-ordination.

What you need:

▶ a lump of clay for each child

▶ hessian or boards

▶ a selection of objects, such as plastic straws, buttons, string, matchsticks and corks

▶ water to keep clay moist

▶ labels and newspaper

▶ a safe place for drying models.

Suggestions:

▶ Collect a wide range of objects of different sizes and shapes. Make sure some are long, such as straws; add softer, pliable objects, such as string; little things like seeds and pasta stars; and things with holes, such as beads, macaroni etc.

► Although the children will be able to carry out this activity independently, for safety reasons it may be necessary to supervise younger or less reliable children, to prevent accidental swallowing while using small items such as buttons or pebbles.

What you do:

1. Put a piece of hessian or some boards on the table.

2. Give each child a lump of clay to play with and manipulate.

3. Put a selection of materials in separate containers and invite the children to choose some items to add to their clay.

4. Encourage the children to push the materials into the clay so they remain there when the clay has hardened.

5. Put a name label underneath each creation.

6. Leave the clay to dry for approximately 48 hours.

More little ideas...

► When the sculptures are dry, spray them with gold or silver paint. This makes a wonderful Christmas display.

► Try making a joint sculpture with all the children by putting a whole bag of clay in a builder's tray and working on it as a group. You could do this after a walk in the park or the country.

► When complete, you could mount the sculpture on a board (using nails or strong glue), spray or paint it and hang it on the wall.

► Ask parents or local hardware stores for leftover nuts, bolts, screws, wall plugs etc. and use these to make sculptures. Thread washers or beads on wires or strings to add even more interest.

► Before you start adding things, texture the lump of clay with forks, sieves, graters or textured fabrics, then add objects as before.

► Make a mock jungle and use it for small world play.

Measure for measure

Try this activity as a pre-weighing experience. Estimating and guessing weights, and using the language of 'heavier' and 'lighter', will help to consolidate the concept.

What you need:

▶ a large lump of damp clay

▶ plastic knives

▶ some simple scales (for older children).

Suggestions:

▶ Don't use this activity too early as a teaching session! Give the children plenty of time with adult support to explore the difficult concepts involved in weight and mass.

▶ Children also need time to experiment with dividing lumps of clay, using simple cutting implements. These should include blunt metal knives (old school dining knives or butter knives are ideal). Plastic knives are often too brittle for this job and may shatter, leaving sharp edges. Even the youngest children should be taught how to use appropriate cutting implements safely.

What you do:

1. Give each child some clay and talk about ways of cutting or breaking it into several pieces. Don't worry if the clay pieces are different sizes – this will make the activity more interesting.

2. Look at the pieces of clay together. Ask questions, such as 'How many pieces are there?' and 'Can any be cut in half again?' Use mathematical language (bigger/smaller, same/different, size/shape, heavy/light, heavy/heavier/heaviest etc.) as you hold the pieces in your hands and pass them to each other.

3. Now introduce the idea of comparing two pieces of clay – ask questions such as 'Which is the biggest/heaviest piece?' and 'Which is smaller/lighter?'

4. With older, more experienced children, you could introduce a simple balance scale and experiment with pieces of clay in each side. Remember, the use of standard weights is not necessary for this age; the concepts of weight and mass are much more important.

More little ideas...

▶ Leave simple scales out for free play with marbles, beads, pasta etc., but be aware that small children might put these items in their mouths.

▶ Make some 'parcels' of different sizes and weights for a 'Heavier or Lighter?' game. Include some parcels that are big and light or small and heavy, so children really have to think about size and weight being different.

Making models

Self-hardening clay is ideal for beginners to use in making models. It is strong, easy to use and quick to complete, needing no firing to make it durable.

What you need:

▶ a piece of clay
▶ hessian squares or boards
▶ rolling pins and safe knives
▶ water to keep clay moist
▶ card for labels
▶ a safe place for drying models
▶ newspaper
▶ paints and brushes
▶ dilute PVA glue to glaze.

Suggestions:

▶ Before you begin this sort of activity, make sure the children have had plenty of free experience with clay. Making models takes time and persistence.

- You could look in books at animals and characters from stories to see how they look and how their bodies are shaped.

- Self-hardening clay has tiny nylon fibres mixed in the clay. When you paint hardener on the model, the fibres become stiff and support the clay, making it more resistant to knocks and cracks.

- Talk to the children about modelling from the big lump of clay rather than sticking bits on!

- When making models, it sometimes helps to prop them with crumpled newspaper, card rolls or other bits of clay until the model sets. Children may need help with this technique.

What you do:

1. Talk about what the children would like to model with the clay.

2. Put a piece of hessian or board on the table for each child.

3. Let each child take their own lump of clay and stay with them as they mould it to the desired shape, using tools if they wish.

4. Let the children work alone, but be available if they get stuck or need help.

5. When they are satisfied with their creations, put a name label underneath the model and place it in an area where it can dry without being disturbed.

6. Leave the models to dry for approximately 48 hours.

7. When dry, talk about how the models have hardened. Then decorate as the children wish.

More little ideas...

- Leave books and pictures so the children can see them as they work.

- Visit a museum or art gallery to look at sculpture, collage and other models. Look carefully at how the limbs and other parts are fixed, and how the clay is smoothed over the joints.

Beside the seaside

Try this way of using the shells and other seaside collections children bring after the holidays. The different sizes, shapes and textures all provide opportunities for language development and manipulation.

What you need:

- ▶ a lump of clay for each child
- ▶ a selection of small shells, pebbles, dried seaweed, driftwood, twigs, sand etc.
- ▶ hessian or boards
- ▶ rolling pins, plastic knives and lolly sticks
- ▶ water to keep clay moist.

Suggestions:

- ▶ You could use this activity as either a permanent or a fleeting experience. If you want to keep the pictures as a permanent feature, they will need to be protected by coating with dilute PVA once dry. However, you might rather use the activity for a non-permanent exploration of seaside objects. Whichever you decide, tell the children first.

What you do:

1. Examine the shells and other items that have been collected and invite the children to make a picture to remind them of the seaside.

2. Put a piece of hessian or board on the table.

3. Give each child a lump of clay and suggest that they roll it flat using the rolling pin (to about 1cm thick).

4. Press four lolly sticks into the clay to form a rough square.

5. Using a plastic knife, cut any clay that is outside the square and remove the lolly sticks.

6. Let each child select a few pieces from the seashore collection.

7. Press the pieces gently into the clay square. Talk about the picture before returning the objects to the collection and rolling up the clay.

8. If you want the pictures to be permanent, you could write the child's name in the clay with a stick or clay tool.

9. Place the pictures in an area where they will not be disturbed.

10. Leave to dry for approximately 48 hours before painting or glazing with PVA.

More little ideas...

▶ Try making collages in trays or plant saucers of damp sand. Use natural objects from walks and visits. Make a permanent record by photographing the collage of each child.

▶ Make a big seaside collage in a builder's tray of damp sand. Add some small world sea creatures, such as crabs, starfish, small fish, seahorses, limpets etc.

Glorious mud!

Children love playing with mud and getting dirty, but for many of them it is forbidden territory. Provide this enjoyable experience in the security of your setting.

What you need:

▶ aprons or old clothes

▶ a small patch of land that can be dug and played in; choose a shady spot or put up a gazebo over the area on sunny days

▶ small garden tools, such as spades, trowels, rakes and small buckets

▶ water.

Suggestions:

▶ Always check any area the children are going to use. Make sure there are no hazards, such as sharp stones or other debris. Barefoot experiences should always be carried out in new sterilised compost bought from a garden centre or other supplier; otherwise children should wear old shoes or wellington boots.

▶ This is a messy activity, so make sure the children are wearing old clothes, or are well covered up.

▶ In dry weather, you may need to soften the ground with water ahead of time.

What you do:

1. Put the tools and water containers in baskets near the muddy area, so the children can reach them easily.

2. Encourage them to explore the muddy area with their hands, and with their feet too if they are not wearing wellies.

3. Make sure that children have easy and free access to the tools and containers so that they can use them when they are ready.

4. The children will need very little support and will soon be digging holes and channels, making mud pies and filling up buckets.

5. Make sure the children have positive messages from adults about this experience. It is very easy to convey by your expression, body language or words that you disapprove of the activity or don't like mess!

6. Provide buckets or bowls of water, or access to a hose or outside tap, for children to wash themselves and their tools at the end of their play.

More little ideas...

▶ Tip a bucket of soil on a large sheet of plastic and examine it together. Encourage the children to look closely at the soil and feel it with their fingers. Look for tiny insects and other objects.

▶ If you are fortunate enough to have a gentle slope in the outdoor area, make part of it into a mud slide. It will provide hours of amusement and children will be learning first hand about forces and gravity. After wet weather, when the ground is soft, dig out any grass and smooth over the mud ready for sliding in boots!

Snow

Snow is a 'first time' event for many young children, so if it does snow, put your plans on hold and go outside to enjoy it.

What you need:

▶ snow
▶ wellies or weatherproof shoes
▶ warm clothes
▶ an empty water tray
▶ magnifying glasses
▶ buckets and other containers for collecting snow.

Suggestions:

▶ Some children may not have weatherproof clothing, so make sure they don't get chilled outside as they collect the snow. Remember young children lose body heat rapidly, even when they are on the move.

- Collect pairs of spare wellington boots for days when it rains or snows. Children often come to school in clothing or shoes that are not suitable for experiencing our changeable weather. No child should be prevented from experiencing an activity because they have come in unsuitable clothing.

- Buy some cheap waterproof clothing for your setting. You will be surprised how often you use it!

What you do:

1. When there has been a snowfall, go outside to experience it together.

2. Hold small pieces of snow and watch and feel it melt. Mould the snow into snowballs and throw them at the fence or wall.

3. Roll snow and watch it grow in a big ball, then make a snowman.

4. Look at the footprints that have been made by humans, animals and birds. Try to guess who made each set of prints.

5. Make more prints by running into fresh snow, and follow them back again. Jump and hop to see the prints you make.

6. If the snow is still falling, use magnifying glasses to look closely at individual snowflakes as they fall on clothing or gloves.

Or explore snow indoors:

1. Take enough snow indoors to fill up a water tray or large container.

2. Explore the snow and watch it melt and turn into water.

More little ideas...

- Put some small world people and polar animals in the snow for an unusual small world play session.

- Make snow angels by lying down in the snow and moving your arms up and down to make an imprint of wings. Get up carefully and look at the angel print you have made.

Soap Snow

Models made with soap snow will set into solid shapes that last for several weeks. You could also use soap snow to make a snowscape for a temporary small world.

What you need:

Per 4 children

▶ 4 cups of soapflakes (available in most supermarkets)

▶ rotary or balloon whisks

▶ large shallow tray or bowl

▶ 2 cups of water.

Suggestions:

▶ This activity generates lots of conversation about how things change when mixed. Use the opportunity to talk with the children about what is happening as they work, both when mixing the snow and when playing with it.

▶ Mop up any snow that falls on the floor, to avoid slipping. Have a supply of old towels or newspaper handy, or do the activity outside, ideally on the grass.

▶ Warn the children not to get the snow in their eyes – it won't do any damage, but it will sting!

What you do:

1. Put a bowl of warm water for rinsing hands near the 'snow' tray.
2. Put the soap flakes and water in the tray.
3. Use a whisk to mix the water and soapflakes together.
4. Add more soapflakes or water as needed to make a thick consistency (similar to whipped cream).
5. Dip your hands into warm water to avoid the soap snow sticking to them and play with the snow, making it into peaks and mountains, smoothing and patting it. Try holding it in your hands and squeezing or shaping it.
6. Let the children have plenty of free play time with the snow before suggesting that you keep the shapes!

   ▷ Sculpt the foam into shapes and figures.

   ▷ Leave to set hard on card or boards. The shapes won't last for ever, but they will stay firm for several weeks.

More little ideas...

▶ Cut the side from a large cardboard box (the bigger the better!). Cover it with soap snow to create a base for a snowy scene. Leave to dry hard, then add small figures or toys – penguins, snowmen, people, boats, sledges etc.

▶ Make little snow scenes on cards for Christmas greetings.

Craft clay

This recipe for craft clay is quick to make and creates a dough that is easy to shape. It can be used just for the experience or can be made into models for painting later.

What you need:

▶ aprons
▶ 1 cup of cornflour
▶ 2 cups of bicarbonate of soda
▶ 1 $^1/_4$ cups of water
▶ food colouring (optional)
▶ saucepan
▶ damp cloth
▶ rolling pins.

Suggestions:

▶ This recipe is best made without the children up to step 7, as it involves cooking. The resulting dough is very smooth and pleasant to use, so it's worth the extra effort.

▶ If you want more recipes for dough, including many which the children can make unaided, look at **The Little Book of Dough**.

What you do:

1. Measure all the ingredients into a saucepan.
2. If you want coloured dough, mix food colouring with the water before you add it to the mixture.
3. Cook gently over a medium heat.
4. Stir the mixture all the time as it begins to thicken.
5. Allow to cool slightly and stir thoroughly again. If it is too thick to stir, tip it out and knead with your hands.
6. Leave to cool under a damp cloth.
7. Knead again.
8. Give each child a good lump of dough and encourage free play. Offer some simple tools – sticks, clay tools, cutters, garlic press etc.
9. If the children want to keep their creations, put them somewhere to dry or bake them in a low oven till hard right through. Then paint and varnish.
10. This dough is good for making pretend food for shops, domestic play, or role-play situations. You could make burgers, chips, peas, buns, cakes, jam tarts etc. When painted and varnished, they will be strong enough for long-term use.

More little ideas...

▶ Use animal or vehicle cutters to make mobiles and collages. Cut shapes and, before baking, push a pencil through to make a hole for hanging. For a collage, cut shapes out, bake, paint and varnish, then stick to a big piece of card for display.

Cornflour magic

Mixing cornflour with a little water makes an unusual texture that feels both wet and dry. Children will be fascinated by how it moves and changes.

What you need:

I will need

- aprons
- 1 packet of cornflour
- a plate or small tray for each child
- water – preferably in a small jug for each child.

Suggestions:

- This can be a messy activity, but is really worth the effort, as children will be fascinated by how the mixture moves about.

- Cornflour washes out of clothes very easily, but when you clear away, don't be tempted to try to wash the spills off tables etc. with water – you'll be there forever. Try using an old credit card or store loyalty card to scrape the dots and lumps off surfaces. Children will love to help!

What you do:

1. Give each child a plate or small tray.

2. Half fill a small jug with water.

3. If the children want coloured water, let them add a few drops of food colouring.

4. Let them spoon about two tablespoons of cornflour on each plate.

5. Add the water a little at a time.

6. Encourage the children to mix the water into the cornflour a bit at a time with their fingers.

7. Talk with them about how the cornflour changes when water is added and what it feels like.

8. Stay near while they start to move the mixture around with their fingers and hands.

9. If the mixture becomes too wet, add a little more cornflour. If it becomes too dry, then add more water.

More little ideas...

▶ Mix two packets of cornflour and approximately two cups of coloured water in a large container. Add some food colouring if you wish. Encourage the children to play as a group.

▶ Mixing sand, cornflour and PVA together will make a thick clay that is suitable for sculpting or moulding into permanent models.

Finger paint

Finger paint is a great way for children to relax and feel calm. Give them plenty of time to explore the activity unhurried.

What you need:

- ▶ aprons
- ▶ 1/2 cup of cornflour
- ▶ 1 tablespoon of sugar
- ▶ 1 teaspoon of salt
- ▶ 2 cups of cold water
- ▶ food colouring
- ▶ saucepan and wooden spoon
- ▶ a clean, washable surface
- ▶ teaspoon.

Suggestions:

- ▶ Make plenty of this mixture ahead of time. Add a range of different food colourings to small quantities and store them in airtight containers in a cool place until you need them. They will keep for several months.

▶ Keep the activity for free play for plenty of time, before making any suggestion of taking prints of the designs.

What you do: ———————————————————

To prepare the colours:

1. Mix all the ingredients together in the saucepan.
2. Heat over a low heat for about 10 to 15 minutes.
3. Keep stirring the mixture until it is smooth and thick.
4. Take the pan off the heat and let the mixture cool.
5. Add a few drops of food colouring to the mixture and stir.
6. Repeat the process for other colours.

The activity:

1. Work with one or two children at a time.
2. Pour some of the 'paint' onto the table and let the children explore, touch and feel.
3. Encourage them to move the mixture around with their fingers and hands.
4. Make lines, squiggles, patterns and pictures.

More little ideas...

▶ When the child is pleased with their finger painting, try taking a print. Lay a piece of thin paper over the painted area and rub gently with your hands (the child can help too). Now gently peel the paper off the table and you will have a print. Leave to dry. The salt in the paint will make it sparkle when it is dry.

▶ Try offering more than one colour at a time for an experiment in colour mixing. More than two colours is usually disappointing!

Squirty cream

Shaving cream and dairy cream are two aerosol products that give different textures and sensory experiences. Use either, but younger children may be better off with edible cream. You don't need much, so it's not as extravagant as it may seem to have some good fun and a magical time.

What you need:

▶ aprons

▶ a can of shaving foam or edible dairy cream

▶ a clear, washable surface.

I will need

Suggestions:

▶ Get bargain shaving cream from budget stores. Make sure it is fragrance free and hypoallergenic. This way, all children should be able to use it safely. However, before any malleable activity, check your records for skin allergies and any other allergic reactions.

▶ It is safer to use edible cream with younger children. Don't use both foams together without telling children clearly which sort they are using – they may try eating it, and need a warning. Younger children should be supervised in this activity.

What you do:

1. Work with pairs or threes. Although the children will be able to carry out this activity independently, for safety reasons it will be necessary to supervise to avoid foam or cream getting into their eyes.

2. Squirt a mound of the foam or cream on to the surface next to each child, and a mound for you.

3. Get involved as they move it around using fingers and hands, feeling the texture. Talk about the texture and look of the foam.

4. Model using your fingers to make patterns and pictures in the foam or cream.

5. Add more if the foam begins to dissolve or the cream turns runny.

More little ideas...

▶ Try using plastic combs and rakes to make patterns.

▶ Put a little finger paint or other colouring near the edge of the foam and see what happens as the children incorporate this into their play. Talk about what happens.

▶ Make hard and soft feelie bags by putting objects into two draw-string bags. Ask the children to feel each object, guess what it is and talk about the different textures. For the soft bag, try objects such as a teddy, a sponge or a feather. For the hard bag, include objects such as a fir cone, an eggcup or a plastic toy.

Shiny, slimy soap flakes

A different use of soap flakes in this softer, more liquid form gives children practice in pouring, whisking, scooping, filling and emptying. The mixture moves in a slow motion and makes fine movements easier to control.

What you need:

- ▶ half a packet of soap flakes
- ▶ 1 large container, such as a water tray or baby bath
- ▶ 2 litres of warm water
- ▶ balloon or rotary whisks
- ▶ kitchen tools such as scoops, spoons, cups, funnels and sponges
- ▶ plastic bottles or containers.

I will need

Suggestions:

- ▶ You may have to search a bit for soap flakes, but the search is really worth it!
- ▶ Warn the children about getting the mixture in their eyes; it won't do lasting damage, but it will sting.

What you do:

1. Using a spoon, let the children help to mix the warm water into the soap flakes (it will look a bit lumpy at this stage).

2. Leave to stand for an hour or so, until it becomes solid.

3. Add more water if it has become too thick.

4. Give the children whisks and beaters to mix again.

5. Encourage the children to play with their hands at first before introducing the tools and plastic bottles, funnels, sieves etc.

6. Talk about how the mixture changes and what it feels like. Encourage the children to think of words to describe it and have fun making up words together, such as 'squidgy' or 'slimy'. Children will be able to play independently, but you can encourage language development if you work with them.

More little ideas...

▶ Add a few drops of lavender oil or other aromatherapy oils to make a fragrant mixture. (Check for allergies before using oils.)

▶ After playing, use the soap flakes mixture to hand-wash some of the dolls' clothes. Just add some more warm water and take the bowl outside for some more fun.

▶ Put a bar of soap in a shallow bowl of water, so that children can watch it dissolve. Talk about how it looks and how it feels.

▶ Watch to see if other things dissolve in water – try salt, sugar, flour, sand, washing powder, instant coffee and mud. Encourage the children to guess whether each solid will or won't dissolve. Children can experiment themselves using small clear containers of their own.

Bean feast!

Dried pulses, pasta, seeds and lentils provide a very satisfying experience when provided in quantity. The bigger the quantity, the better the experience.

What you need:

▶ a protective sheet or newspaper for the floor or table
▶ a water tray, baby bath or builder's tray
▶ a quantity of dried lentils, peas, pasta, rice or sunflower seeds
▶ kitchen equipment such as scoops, spoons, ladles, cup measures and funnels
▶ dustpan and brush.

Suggestions:

▶ Children can experience this activity independently. Just check that they know about not putting the objects in their mouths, ears etc.
▶ Avoid using red kidney beans as they can be toxic when dry.

- When the children have finished playing, use the bean and seed mixture to feed the birds.

- Try supermarkets and cash and carry stores for really big quantities at bargain prices. This is a good investment as you can use the materials over and over again.

- You can just use one type at a time or mix the sorts.

What you do:

1. Let the children help you to choose a dried food and tip it into your deep tray or bowl.

2. All plunge your hands into the food and feel the sensation of it moving through your fingers and over your hands.

3. Offer the children the kitchen tools when they are ready.

4. Encourage them to mix, measure, stir and pour, then you can leave them to it!

5. Sweep up spillages with a dustpan and brush to prevent slipping.

6. Children may need help in using some of the utensils. Make sure you offer a good range of sizes and types of tools and implements.

More little ideas...

- Try a 'self-service salad bar' – fill individual margarine tubs with lentils, peas and seeds, and give each child an empty tub to fill. Remind the children not to eat the pulses.

- Bury small objects in the dried food, such as corks or wooden blocks. Ask the children to search for the objects and try to guess what they are touching before bringing it to the surface.

- Fill up a shallow tray with bird seed and invite the children to take off their socks and shoes and stand in it. Talk about what it feels like.

- Don't let the seeds get wet or they may sprout – although, of course, that would provide another great activity!

Spaghetti or jelly

Slippery cooked spaghetti and shiny jelly both provide tactile experiences with an added benefit of developing muscular control. Don't offer both at the same time!

What you need:

- ▶ aprons
- ▶ a protective sheet or newspaper for the floor or table
- ▶ a large deep tray or washing up-bowl
- ▶ cooked and cooled spaghetti
- ▶ food colouring (optional) or 3 packets of jelly
- ▶ 3 small bowls for the jelly
- ▶ a table knife.

Suggestions:

- ▶ Any type of pasta will work, but spaghetti has a unique feel. Just remember to add a little oil to it when cooked, to stop it sticking together.

▶ Adding food colouring creates a different experience. Try black spaghetti or different coloured stars or pasta shapes.

▶ Make the jelly in separate bowls, some with a bit less water to make it a different texture. Tip it all out together for play.

What you do:

1. Cook the pasta according to the instructions. Make sure it is 'al dente' for a more robust material. Add food colouring to the water before or during cooking. If using jelly, make it up according to the packet instructions.

2. Put a plastic sheet or newspaper on the table and put the cooked spaghetti or roughly chopped jelly into a deep tray or bowl.

3. Using their hands, the children can move the spaghetti/jelly around, squeezing and pummelling it, watching how it moves. Encourage them to push their hands into the stuff, feeling, touching and smelling it.

4. Encourage them to talk about and describe the food. Introduce new words such as 'shiny', 'slimy' and 'slippery'.

More little ideas...

▶ Offer this activity in your domestic play area, so children can use it with saucepans, plates and bowls for pretend meals. It's a great way to develop fine motor skills.

▶ Try making pictures with cooked spaghetti. Cook in the usual way, but don't add any oil. Drain the spaghetti in a colander and drop strands onto dark coloured paper. The starch in the spaghetti will make it stick to the paper and, when it is dry, it will harden to make a 'white on black' collage or picture. These look great sprayed gold or silver.

Breakfast cereals

Don't throw those half empty boxes of cereal away when they pass their 'best before' date... use them for another tactile experience.

What you need:

▶ a protective sheet or newspaper for the floor or table

▶ a builder's tray or washing-up bowl

▶ cereal such as Weetabix, or ground coffee and tea

▶ small world toys, such as people, animals or dinosaurs

▶ dustpan and brush.

Suggestions:

▶ Ask parents to send in cereals that are past their sell by date. Sugar-coated varieties are **not** recommended for this activity – they are too tempting for children.

▶ Try saving tea leaves and coffee granules. Dried out, these provide another unusual medium for children to explore. Peg tea bags on a line to dry before emptying (children love doing this!). Dry coffee granules on a tray in a warm place or in a low oven.

▶ Always warn children not to eat the materials or even put them in their mouths. For this reason, you may decide not to use this idea with younger children.

What you do:

1. Put a plastic sheet or newspaper on the table to help when clearing away.

2. Put your chosen ingredients (or some bowls of different ingredients) in a tray or a washing-up bowl.

3. Offer some baskets of different types of small world toys – dinosaurs, farm or zoo animals, small world people, vehicles etc. Or try offering small paper or plastic bags, pots, scoops and funnels for filling and emptying. Encourage the children to play imaginatively together, selecting their own equipment and toys. A vegetable rack is a useful way to store a range of small equipment.

4. Remind the children to sweep up any spillages with the dustpan and brush as they work.

More little ideas...

▶ Fill a tray with coffee, tea or cereal and bury some metal objects. Give the children some magnets to search for the objects.

▶ Make a base board road, park, garden or farm for small world play by painting sections of a big piece of card with dilute PVA glue and sprinkling tea, coffee or crushed cereal on the sections to create roads, fields, ponds etc. Spray your finished layout with clear varnish for added protection, and play away!

Compost

Buy a bag of compost or a growbag from a garden centre or DIY store and have an unusual play experience for all your senses.

What you need:

- aprons
- a large bag of peat or garden compost, such as a growbag
- a large container
- sand play tools, such as spades, small buckets and sand moulds.

Suggestions:

- As with mud play, you should take care that the compost is sterilised and new. Growbags cost very little, especially at the end of summer, so invest in a few for use in the winter when you may not be able to provide such a wide range of outdoor experiences.

- ▶ Check for allergies and sensitive skin before using compost. Some children may need to wear gloves to protect their hands.

- ▶ Always warn children not to eat the materials (or even taste them).

What you do:

1. Tip the compost into a container that is large enough for four children to use (such as a water tray or baby bath).

2. Remove any rough twigs or bark.

3. Let the children help to break down any lumps in the compost with their hands and rake through.

4. Encourage the children to feel the texture of the compost, delving their hands into it and moving it around. Make this a 'hands only' stage.

5. When children have had lots of time to explore, offer the toys or tools usually used for sand, such as spades, rakes, shovels, trowels and sieves.

6. To change the texture of the compost, add a litre or so of water and leave it to be absorbed for about ten minutes.

7. Again, let the children use their hands to feel the sensation of the wet compost when pummelled and squeezed.

8. Now you could introduce the sand moulds so that the children can make shapes.

More little ideas...

- ▶ Hide root vegetables (carrots, swedes, turnips, small potatoes etc.) in damp compost for the children to find and hide again.

- ▶ Grow tomatoes or other vegetables in the compost when the children have finished playing.

Toilet tissue medium

Toilet tissue is a medium with a different texture, and can be used for small world play or collages. Search out a cheap supply in pound shops or other bargain shops.

What you need:

▶ aprons
▶ rolls of toilet tissue
▶ water
▶ a bucket
▶ a colander or sieve.

Suggestions:

▶ If you wish to be ecologically friendly, use tissue made from recycled materials. This will be marked on the packet. Other toilet tissue, especially in white rolls, has often been produced using chemicals that are not environmentally friendly.

What you do:

1. Get the children to help you to tear the toilet tissue into fairly small pieces – about 2cm square.

2. Soak the pieces in a bucket of water for about five minutes.

3. Drain the water out of the paper through a colander or sieve, pressing the paper down firmly.

4. Now squeeze with your hands to remove more water.

5. Mould and form the damp toilet tissue paper into shapes.

6. For a more permanent model, add PVA to the paper when it has been drained and mix in well. This will make a substance that hardens on the surface, although bigger models will probably take a long time to dry all the way through.

More little ideas...

▶ This is another material that is good for making three dimensional base boards for small world play. You can build the white toilet tissue medium up on a base board to make a snow scene, or make a moonscape for rockets and spacemen. If you like, you can paint or spray the scene after it has dried.

▶ Use the medium to make individual pictures for greeting cards or calendars. You can colour the mixture with food colouring or paint.

▶ Make a big group collage on a wooden board. Push buttons, beads, sequins, ribbon etc. into the wet medium, leave to dry thoroughly right through, then coat with spray varnish and hang on a wall.

▶ Make some paintings for the walls of your home corner by using the medium in old picture frames.

Porridge

What better place for a 'Goldilocks and the Three Bears' retelling in small world version! Dry porridge oats can be easily shaped and built into a variety of scenes. Adding water makes another change.

What you need:

▶ aprons
▶ a tray or bowl for each child
▶ 500g of porridge for each child
▶ small world toys.

Suggestions:

▶ Buy big bags of porridge from cash and carry stores so you get the best price. As long as you don't let it get wet, you can use the porridge again and again.

What you do:

1. Giving each child their own tray will encourage them to use their imagination, creating make-believe worlds as well as recreating traditional tales such as 'Goldilocks'. They could shape a porridge landscape: trees, a cottage and paths.

2. Put the porridge into a tray or bowl for each child.

3. Using their hands, the children can flatten, stir, sprinkle or sift the porridge, moving it about in the container.

4. When they have explored the porridge on its own, introduce a range of small world toys, such as people, animals, dinosaurs or cars. Small diggers are great in porridge!

5. Encourage the children to create an imaginary world in their own tray, and perhaps join their trays to each other's with cardboard tubes or strips.

More little ideas...

▶ Add some water to the porridge and see what happens to the texture and handling.

▶ Make a mixture of porridge, flour and water to form a soft modelling dough with an unusual texture.

▶ Encourage the children to tell stories about their worlds. They could do this at group time, taking turns to tell a story.

▶ Tip a large amount of porridge in a builder's tray and walk in it with bare feet. Then add some water and walk about again.

▶ Sing: **Pease porridge hot; pease porridge cold;**
Pease porridge in the pot, nine days old!
Some like it hot; some like it cold;
Some like it in the pot, nine days old!

Sawdust

Sawdust is a good, free material which smells wonderful when wet. Read the safety suggestions before using.

What you need:

- aprons
- a large bag of sawdust, sold as pet bedding
- a large container
- toys and tools used for sand play
- moulds, yoghurt pots and plant pots.

Suggestions:

- Sawdust can be used as an alternative to sand and is widely available from pet stores.

► You need to be aware of the slight risks of using dry sawdust. Based on the ASE Health and Safety Guidance, we would advise that dry sawdust should be used out of doors, so any fine dust is blown away. If you choose to use sawdust indoors, you should add water to damp the dust.

► Check for asthma and other breathing difficulties before using dry sawdust.

What you do:

1. Tip sawdust into a container that is large enough for four children to use (a builder's tray or baby bath is ideal).

2. Run your fingers through the sawdust and remove any rough pieces.

3. Using their hands, the children can feel the texture of the sawdust as they move it around.

4. The sawdust can be played with in this dry state, adding toys or tools used for sand if desired.

5. To change the texture, or for use indoors, add a litre or so of water and leave to absorb for about ten minutes.

6. Again, use hands to feel the sensation of the wet sawdust when pummelled and squeezed.

7. Introduce the moulds so that the children can make shapes, or diggers and dumper trucks for construction play.

More little ideas...

► If you add PVA to damp sawdust, it can be sculpted or moulded into simple shapes and models that will set hard when left to dry.

► Make a collage with sawdust and wood shavings by sticking bits of wood together and adding sawdust and shavings for decoration. Get offcuts of wood from your local timber merchant or DIY store.

► Examine a log together. Touch and smell it, talk about the growth rings and how a log can be a home to insects. Introduce new words such as 'bark', and 'twigs'. Go outdoors and look at different trees.

Paper pulp

Making recycled paper is a time-consuming process, but making the pulp for it is fairly quick and easy, and young children love playing with it.

What you need:

▶ aprons
▶ newspapers or waste paper
▶ water
▶ a large container
▶ potato mashers
▶ newspaper to protect
   the floor.

Suggestions:

▶ Newspaper is ideal for this activity, as is waste paper.
   Magazines or junk mail printed on shiny paper is not so good as it isn't so absorbent.

- Ask parents and friends to keep old newspapers for use in your setting.

- Adding non-fungicidal wallpaper paste will turn this pulp into papier mâché, which can be used to make models, bowls, cups and other containers.

What you do:

1. Spread newspaper on the floor to save time when clearing up any spillages. Talk to the children about what you are going to do.

2. Together, tear the paper into fairly small pieces, about 2cm square.

3. Place in a bucket and add water.

4. Soak overnight, or longer if using strong paper such as computer paper. The longer the paper is left to soak, the easier it will mash. Friday is a good day to start this activity!

5. Pour the paper pulp into a large container, such as a builder's tray.

6. Use the potato mashers to pulp the paper until it begins to break down and resemble porridge.

7. Use fingers and hands to poke, pummel and squeeze the pulp.

8. Talk about the texture and feel of the pulp and how it moves.

More little ideas...

- Squeeze out most of the water from the pulp and add some PVA glue. Use this mixture to make a textured surface on card or boxes.

- Use strips of torn newspaper on black card to create an effective collage.

- Try using strips of stiff paper or card and only sticking the ends down, so you build a creation of bridges and loops, twists and spirals, weaving the paper or card in and out. If you paint the card with stripes of different colours before cutting it into strips, it makes the construction even more exciting to make and to look at.

Making magic

Making magic potions is a traditional childhood activity. Set up this activity so children can make mixtures with interesting colours, smells and textures using familiar ingredients.

What you need:

- aprons
- a margarine tub or similar container for each child
- spoons
- a range of ingredients: cornflour, ketchup, shaving foam, water with food colouring, juice – anything goes!
- a builder's tray.

Suggestions:

- You need to talk with the children before this activity, making sure they understand what they can do and reminding them that they should not drink the potions or give them to anyone else to drink. If you are concerned about the risk, limit the ingredients to edible liquids.

► Try to collect a wide range of little bottles and jars, then can offer small plastic droppers and syringes to fill them.

What you do:

1. Look at the ingredients. Smell each one and look at the colour and texture. Talk about them, using imaginative language and guessing what potion each ingredient could be used for. Try to encourage positive potions that will do good, such as curing a cold, making your hair grow, turning frogs into princes and making you funny or strong.

2. Now offer the containers and ingredients for free play.

3. Help them (if they need it) to mix chosen ingredients together one at a time, using the droppers and little spoons.

4. Talk about the smell and texture of the potions and how they change as the children add ingredients.

5. When the children are satisfied with their potion, tip a little out into a tray and use fingers to feel it and manipulate to make patterns.

6. Talk about what the potion will do. Older children may want to label their own bottles and you can offer to write the spell or cure.

More little ideas...

► Another activity is making pretend party drinks. Give the children water, food colourings, droppers and plastic glasses. You could add umbrellas and straws!

► Make fruit juice mixtures for snack time. Offer different juice flavours and colours in jugs so children can make their own mixtures. Add some coloured straws and a few slices of orange or some cherries for a treat.

Wire sculpture

Florist's wire is pliable and easy to work with, so it is ideal for young children to use for making shapes and structures. Anything with a hole in it can be threaded on as decoration.

What you need:

▶ thin wire, bought from a florist or hardware store
▶ wire cutters or scissors
▶ beads and buttons
▶ clay for a base for the sculpture.

Suggestions:

▶ Don't panic at the suggestion of using wire! Many settings do it. You just need to be careful and remind the children about safety rules. This is a supervised activity until you are sure the children can work safely without you.

- Check the wire before buying to make sure it bends and holds its shape when bent.

- Collect a range of beads, buttons, sequins, corks, shells, pebbles and pasta shapes. Cut lengths of straws etc. with holes big enough for threading.

What you do: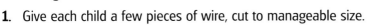

1. Give each child a few pieces of wire, cut to manageable size.

2. Help them to bend the wire into different forms, shaping and re-shaping.

3. Offer beads and buttons for those children who want to thread them on to the wire models.

4. Don't insist (or even suggest) that the creation should represent a person or animal. Abstract sculptures are usually best for beginners. Natural forms such as trees and plants are easier than animals and people.
   You can use fabric pieces or buttons for flowers and add leaves of paper or fabric.

5. Make a firm base for the sculpture by sticking the wire into a lump of clay or plasticine.

More little ideas...

- For a more substantial sculpture, cut some strips of paper or thin fabric, dip these in a PVA/water mixture and bind round the wire. Continue wrapping till the wire is covered. Leave to dry.

- Use flexible wire coat hangers to make simple mobiles. Thread beads and buttons, pasta shapes or other items with holes on lengths of wire or string and fix these to the straight wire at the bottom of the hanger. Add feathers, strips of fabric, ribbon or natural objects such as leaves or flowers.

Turf

Dig up a piece of turf and bring it indoors. You may be very surprised at how long children will spend absorbed in playing with it.

What you need:

I will need

▶ a piece of turf as big as you can manage

▶ a water tray or builder's tray

▶ old kitchen forks and spoons

▶ sticks, clay tools or other things to poke and prod

▶ magnifying glasses

▶ bug pots

▶ a camera (optional).

Suggestions:

▶ This activity has a risk attached. You need to be as sure as you can that the turf is from a clean area of land. The best way is to cut turf from the garden of your setting, bring a square from your own garden, or ask a friend or neighbour if you can borrow a square for a day or two. This way you can check whether the turf has been recently sprayed, exposed to other chemicals or has been fouled by pets.

▶ You could also give the turf a good spray to ensure the grass is fresh.

▶ When you dig up the turf, include a layer of soil under the roots of the grass. This way, there will be some some minibeasts for the children to watch.

What you do:

1. Put the turf, grass side up, in a water tray or builder's tray.

2. Leave the tools and implements in a basket or box beside the tray and allow the children to explore independently.

3. Encourage the children to use the forks and other implements to poke and prise the turf apart so they can see how the grass grows down into the soil.

4. Stay near, so you can join the conversations and explorations, helping the children to look for little insects and perhaps capture some for a closer look. Emphasise the importance of careful handling of small creatures and returning them to their homes after you have looked at them.

5. When the children have looked at the grass side of the turf, carefully turn it over and look at the earth underneath.

6. Explore this side with the children, prising bits of earth off and seeing what the children can discover.

More little ideas...

▶ When you have finished with the turf, return it with any minibeasts to the place where you dug it. The turf should fit neatly back into the hole and will grow back in a short time. If the children can come with you to return it, they can look in the hole where the turf came from to see where it fits.

▶ Bring in some clumps of grass, plants or weeds for children to explore in the same way.

Gravel

Gravel is a noisy, heavy, realistic material for children's play. It is a good alternative to sand for diggers and movers.

What you need:

▶ a bag of pea gravel (from a garden centre or DIY store)
▶ diggers, dumper trucks, cranes, lorries of all sizes and types
▶ a large builder's tray
▶ spades, buckets and barrows.

Suggestions:

▶ If your children like digging, and most do, try to get or make a pit or square frame of wood big enough for children to get inside. Perhaps a parent could help you here, or you could get some decking or railway sleepers from a reclamation yard to make a rectangle.

▶ Another idea is to get some large tyres and fill these with gravel for play. Pea gravel works best as it is small and more rounded than some other gravels.

What you do:

1. Make your frame or buy a big tray and tip the bag of gravel in it.
2. Put the trucks and other tools nearby and leave the children to play.
3. Make sure you give children an opportunity to tell others about what they have been doing in this sort of play. There is often a complex story line behind what they play and it is important to recognise and show interest in what they have done.
4. Try adding some sand to the gravel and see how this affects children's play, imaginative response and movement.
5. Sometimes offer the gravel with tools only, not vehicles. Offer spoons and small bags or buckets and scoops or sieves and funnels.

More little ideas...

▶ Get some child-size wheelbarrows, plastic hard hats and reflective waistcoats and offer these as a role-play activity. Add clip-boards and pens, toy mobile phones or badges for them to use and see what happens.

▶ Buy some bigger stones to wheel around in barrows.

▶ Go and look at a building site to find out about diggers, dumper trucks and building materials.

▶ Put some gravel in a shallow tray and spray with water. Look at the gravel through magnifying glasses to see the individual beauty of the stones. Try making a 'pebble fountain' in a tray of sand and pebbles.

▶ Arrange a visit to a garden centre to look at building and garden materials such as paving stones, different gravels, pebbles etc.

Very tiny seeds

Grass seeds and other very tiny seeds behave like sand, or even water, but provide a very different look and feel.

What you need:

▶ bags of grass seed, wild bird food, budgie seed etc.
▶ scoops, funnels, tubes and spoons
▶ little bags and boxes.

Suggestions:

▶ Go to a farm supplies shop or a big garden centre where they sell grass seed by the kilo. This is much cheaper than the sort in boxes.

▶ Buy bird food in bulk at the beginning or the end of the winter when it will probably be cheaper.

▶ Plastic tubing of different thicknesses is a very useful prop for this activity.

What you do:

1. Tip the little seeds into a big bowl or a water tray.

2. Encourage free play without tools first, feeling the seeds running through their fingers, pouring them from hand to hand, scooping them up and letting them fall again.

3. When the children are ready, offer them the tools and equipment you have gathered. Let them select what they want to use. Just stay close enough to make suggestions, encourage language and praise new ideas for using the equipment.

4. If you have used mixed seeds or have mixed more than one sort, ask the children to suggest how you could sort them out again.

More little ideas...

▶ Offer some plastic or cardboard tubes for pouring seeds down, or try guttering or drainpipes.

▶ Try making a seed way (like a water way) from recycled materials and see if you can make the seeds behave like water, running down pipes and tubes.

▶ Try picking up the seeds with tweezers and putting them in bags to develop fine motor control.

▶ Set up a shop with seeds of different sorts, bags, money and a till so children can buy and sell.

▶ Put the seeds in the role-play area to use as pretend food.

▶ When you have finished playing, feed the seeds to the birds or try planting some to see what they grow into!

Dots and strips

This activity uses recycled materials from offices and homes. It is simple, but effective in encouraging imagination.

What you need:

► a deep tray for playing
► dots from hole punches
► strips from computer paper
► shreddings from a paper shredder
► used paper, torn into thin strips
► a dustpan and brush.

Suggestions:

► If you can't get enough dots, make some by using a hole punch on different colours of paper (or paint the paper first with thin paint, either plain or in patterns and stripes). You could also make dots from wrapping paper. Children like doing this and it strengthens their hand muscles.

- ▶ Ask friends who work in offices to save dots and shreddings for you.
- ▶ Look for confetti dots in gift and celebration shops or bargain shops.
- ▶ You could add some paper stars and other shapes.

What you do:

1. Tip the dots, strips etc. into the tray.
2. Leave the children to explore the mixture as they wish.
3. Some children will want to make patterns or sort the shapes. Discuss the shapes and types of items in the mixture.

More little ideas...

- ▶ Stick dots and strips on card to make collages.

- ▶ Stuff small plastic bags with shreddings, fasten the ends with elastic bands and make a game. Put a box or bucket some distance from the players and take turns to throw the bags into the box.

- ▶ Stick the paper scraps down on card to make a collage and, when dry, spatter paint over the sheet. You could put a thin piece of paper over it and rub with the side of a fat crayon to reveal the pattern of the collage.

- ▶ Float dots on a water tray and watch to see how long it takes until they sink.

Icy shapes

Ice is not a very malleable substance, but it is very exciting if presented in an imaginative way.

What you need:

▶ a water tray

▶ aprons

▶ ice shapes, frozen in regular and more unusual moulds and ice trays.

Suggestions:

▶ Keep your eyes open for different shapes of ice trays: hearts, penguins, fish, flowers etc.

▶ Try some of these other shapes for freezing: ice-cream boxes, yogurt pots, egg boxes, bun trays, foil cases, glasses, trays from chocolate boxes and biscuits.

► And some really unusual ones: rubber gloves, sand moulds and wellingtons (use old ones as you may have to cut them to get the ice shape out!).

What you do:

1. Put a small amount of water in the water tray.
2. Tip the ice shapes in and leave for the children to explore.
3. Make sure the children don't get too cold as they play with this new and exciting material. They may wish to wear gloves.

More little ideas...

► Try freezing little things in ice cubes:
beads
sequins
flowers
seeds
lego bricks
buttons
tiny bells
cake decorations.

Warn children about putting small objects in their mouths.

► Add some food colouring to ice shapes and watch what the colouring does as the water freezes, and again as it melts.

► Experiment with freezing other liquids and solids such as milk, yoghurt, fruit and fruit juices.

► Make other foods that change as they cool – jelly, custard and ice cream.

The **Little Books** series consists of:

50
All through the year
Bags, Boxes & Trays
Big Projects
Bricks & Boxes
Celebrations
Christmas
Circle Time
Clay and Malleable
Materials
Clothes and Fabric
Colour, Shape & Number
Cooking from Stories
Cooking Together
Counting
Dance
Dance Music CD
Dens
Discovery Bottles
Dough
Drama from Stories
Explorations
Fine Motor Skills
Free and Found
Fun on a Shoestring
Games with Sounds
Gross Motor Skills
Growing Things
ICT
Investigations
Junk Music

Kitchen Stuff
Language Fun
Light and Shadow
Listening
Living Things
Look and Listen
Making Books and Cards
Making Poetry
Maps and Plans
Mark Making
Maths Activities
Maths from Stories
Maths Outdoors
Maths Problem Solving
Maths Songs & Games
Messy Play
Minibeast Hotels
Multi-sensory Stories
Music
Nursery Rhymes
Opposites
Outdoor Play
Outside in All Weathers
Painting
Parachute Play
Persona Dolls
Phonics
Playground Games
Prop Boxes for Role Play
Props for Writing
Puppet Making

Puppets in Stories
Resistant Materials
Rhythm and Raps
Role Play
Role Play Windows
Sand and Water
Science through Art
Scissor Skills
Seasons
Sequencing Skills
Sewing and Weaving
Small World Play
Sound Ideas
Special Days
Stories from around the
world
Story bags
Storyboards
Storybuilding
Storytelling
Time and Money
Time and Place
Topsy Turvy
Traditional Tales
Treasure Baskets
Treasure Boxes
Tuff Spot Activities
Washing lines
Woodwork
Writing

All available from
www.bloomsbury.com